KANGAROOS

LIVING WILD

Published by Creative Education
P.O. Box 227, Mankato, Minnesota 56002
Creative Education is an imprint of The Creative Company
www.thecreativecompany.us

Design and production by Mary Herrmann
Art direction by Rita Marshall
Printed by Corporate Graphics in the United States of America

Photographs by Alamy (Gerry Pearce, Penny Tweedie), Australian Postal Corporation, Corbis (Michael Amendolia), Dreamstime (Alain, Kitchner Bain, Yong Chen, David Cox, Damerau, Rusty Dodson, Michael Elliott, Adrian Lewart, Marcel Luttmann, Robyn Mackenzie, Ron Sumners, Susinder, Crystal Venus), Getty Images (Tim Graham, Joseph Lycett, Belinda Wright/National Geographic), iStockphoto (Felix Alim, Michelle Allen, Bruce Amos, Carolina Garcia Aranda, Tamara Bauer, Jenny Bonner, John Carnemolla, John M. Chase, Susan Flashman, John Fuller, Nicky Gordon, Pete Karas, Hugh MacDougall, Filip Put, Farzin Salimi, Martti Salmela, Clayton Sharrard, Smiley Joanne, Chris Williams, Lisa Kyle Young)

Library of Congress Cataloging-in-Publication Data
Gish, Melissa.
Kangaroos / by Melissa Gish.
p. cm. — (Living wild)
Includes bibliographical references and index.
Summary: A look at kangaroos, including their habitats, physical characteristics such as the females' pouches, behaviors, relationships with humans, and valued status in the world today.
ISBN 978-1-58341-970-0
1. Kangaroos—Juvenile literature. I. Title. II. Series.

QL737.M35G57 2010
599.2'22—dc22   2009025171

CPSIA: 092611 PO1507

9 8 7 6 5 4 3 2

CREATIVE EDUCATION

KANGAROOS

Melissa Gish

Like an orange ball floating on a sea of grass, the
sun touches the horizon. Here in Australia's

Warrumbungle National Park, kangaroos stand
up and stretch after a hot, lazy afternoon . . .

L

ike an orange ball floating on a sea of grass, the sun touches the horizon. Here in Australia's Warrumbungle National Park, kangaroos stand up and stretch after a hot, lazy afternoon spent sleeping in the shade of scattered trees. As the temperature drops, the kangaroos begin their evening ritual of munching on grass and tender shrubs. A female rises, and her offspring, called a joey, peeks its head out of the pouch on its mother's belly. It stretches out its arms, leans down, and touches the grass with its tiny paws. Then it slips out of the pouch for the first time in its life, hopping in small circles close to its mother, bending to nibble the slender grass, and then leaning back on its tail to practice balancing. Suddenly, a hawk screeches overhead, startling the joey, who quickly leaps head first back into its mother's pouch. It will explore the world again tomorrow.

■ **Eastern Grey Kangaroo** eastern Australia, Tasmania

■ **Western Grey Kangaroo** western and southern Australia

■ **Red Kangaroo** central Australia

■ **Antilopine Kangaroo** northern Australia

■ **Black Walleroo** northern Australia

■ **Common Walleroo** throughout Australia, except for coastal and tropical areas

Kangaroos are native only to the continent of Australia and the island of Tasmania. The six species of kangaroo have adapted to life in the various regions of Australia, with some suited to the drier and warmer plains of central and western areas and others for the more temperate regions of northern and eastern forests. The colored squares represent home territories of each species.

BIG BOUNCING FEET

About 54 members of the Macropodidae family—including kangaroos—live in the open spaces of Australia, New Zealand, New Guinea, and some surrounding islands. Macropods are characterized by their straight cutting teeth, powerful tails, and large hind feet. The family includes the endangered quokka, along with various wallabies, pademelons, and tree kangaroos. It also includes six species of animals that have hind feet measuring 10 inches (25 cm) or longer, leading scientists to commonly group them together as kangaroos.

These six species of kangaroo are the eastern grey, western grey, red, and antilopine kangaroos, and the black and common wallaroos. The name macropod means "large foot" in Latin and Greek, and all macropods, with the exception of tree kangaroos, have large hind feet and long hind legs. The name "kangaroo" is a variation of *gungurru*, a northeast Australian **Aboriginal** word for a kind of kangaroo that is now extinct.

Kangaroos are mammals. All mammals produce milk to feed their young and, with the exceptions of the egg-laying platypuses and echidnas of Australia,

Kangaroos and their relatives are the only animals weighing more than 10 pounds (4.5 kg) that hop as their main form of movement.

While they usually feed on dead animals, Tasmanian devils have been known to attack small kangaroos.

give birth to live offspring. Mammals are also warm-blooded. This means that their bodies try to maintain a healthy, constant temperature that is usually warmer than their surroundings. Kangaroos live in hot climates and cool themselves by licking their front limbs. The saliva **evaporates** to cool the blood just beneath the skin. Kangaroos also pant like dogs, which reduces their internal body temperature.

Kangaroos make up only a fraction of the nearly 300 marsupial species on Earth. The word "marsupial" means "purse bearer." Only female marsupials have the thick folds of flesh on their abdomens where they carry their young throughout development and infancy. Kangaroos are the world's largest marsupials. They share their **Australasian** habitat with smaller marsupials such as the koala, wombat, Tasmanian devil, and banded anteater, which is also known as the numbat.

Male kangaroos are called boomers, and females are called flyers. The red kangaroo is the largest of the kangaroo species. Males weigh up to 200 pounds (90 kg) and stand 6 feet (1.8 m) tall. Their body lengths average five feet (1.5 m), and their tails can add up to four more

Kangaroos have excellent hearing and can make their large, rounded ears pivot to hear sounds from all sides.

Unlike male red kangaroos, females have a pale bluish tint to their fur, causing them to be called "blue-fliers."

feet (1.2 m). Females are smaller, rarely reaching six feet in height (1.8 m). The other kangaroo species are nearly as large as the red but have adopted varying characteristics to suit their environments.

Kangaroo fur, called pelage, is thick and velvety, protecting the kangaroo from thorns and brambles and insulating the animal from the heat of its environment. The grey kangaroos are named for their primary coloring. They also have whitish underparts, black tips on their tails, and fine hair on their jaw, mouth, and nose—the part of an animal's face called a muzzle. The male red kangaroo is a reddish-brown color, while the female is bluish-gray. Red kangaroos have only fine hair on their muzzles. Wallaroos, reddish in color with whitish underparts, have no hair on their muzzles.

All kangaroos are herbivores, meaning they eat only vegetation such as grass, shrubs, and the leaves of small trees. A kangaroo's front teeth, called incisors, are designed for clipping grass close to the ground. The back teeth, called molars, are sharply ridged for grinding food into pulp. Kangaroos have four pairs of molars in each jaw. Constant chewing causes the front molars to wear

Despite having good eyesight, kangaroos tend to respond only to moving objects.

A female kangaroo may also be called a doe or a Jill, and a male kangaroo may be called a buck, Jack, or an old man.

down to the roots and eventually fall out. When this happens, the back molars move forward. By the time a kangaroo is very old—about 18 to 20 years—it may have only one upper and one lower molar left in its mouth.

An adult kangaroo eats about 15 pounds (6.8 kg) of vegetation each day. Digesting so much plant fiber takes a special stomach—one with four chambers, or sections. Food passes through the first chamber, called the rumen, where bacteria and acids soften it. Then the food is regurgitated, or brought back up to the mouth. This food

mass, called a cud, is chewed again. After it is swallowed, the cud is then fully digested. Kangaroos can survive for months without drinking water, as the vegetation they eat provides plenty of moisture. If plants dry out and kangaroos need water, they will dig pits about three feet (.9 m) deep until they reach water.

On a hot day, a kangaroo can drink all the water it needs in a single 30-minute visit to a water source.

Red kangaroos live in central Australia's hot, arid plains, an area known as the "Red Center." Grey and antilopine kangaroos cannot tolerate that much heat, so they live most everywhere else in Australia, where the land is more

Rock wallabies have rough pads of skin on the bottoms of their feet that help them negotiate rocky trails.

Eastern grey and western grey kangaroos sometimes mate with each other, but the offspring they produce are always sterile.

forested. Wallaroos can be found on the rocky landscapes and steep slopes of far northern and northeastern Australia. They rest in caves during the hottest parts of the day.

Because wallaroos rarely travel long distances to forage, their bodies **adapted** by developing shorter, stockier legs than grey and red kangaroos, which may travel more than 100 miles (161 km) to find food if a home territory provides insufficient vegetation. To travel, kangaroos do not run; they jump. The kangaroo's body, with its powerful hind legs and large hind feet, is designed for jumping. About 75 percent of a kangaroo's body weight is located in its hindquarters, which are very muscular. A kangaroo can travel at up to 44 miles (70 km) per hour for short distances, leaping 30 feet (9 m) forward and up to 10 feet high (3 m).

To keep its balance as it bounds forward, the kangaroo raises its heavy tail. Powerful **tendons** in its back legs bounce like springs to allow a kangaroo to hop steadily for hours without tiring. The average speed of a cruising kangaroo is 13 to 16 miles (21-26 km) per hour. Kangaroos also shuffle along slowly by leaning on their front paws and swinging their back legs up together

from underneath them. This is called crawl-walking. The kangaroo has four toes on each hind foot. The two inner toes are partially fused and share a long, sharp claw that is used for grooming and defense. The kangaroo's front paws have five "fingers" with sharp claws that are also used for grooming and for gripping food as well. Kangaroos must spend a lot of time grooming themselves to keep pesky insects out of their fur.

In order to begin hopping, a kangaroo must have its tail on the ground and then lift it to help maintain balance.

Except for the purpose of a zoo exchange, Australian law prohibits the exportation of live kangaroos.

LEAPS AND BOUNDS

Kangaroos are social animals, living in groups called mobs that consist of at least 2 or 3 and can have up to 100 individuals. A dominant male leads the mob, which includes a number of adult females, as well as both male and female juveniles. Every kangaroo knows its place in the mob's **hierarchy**. The head female, usually the oldest and the one charged with teaching younger kangaroos how to get along in the mob, is called the matriarch. A sentry, or lookout, is responsible for staying alert to potential threats and for warning the rest of the mob when danger approaches. Sentries will sound the alarm by thumping the ground with their feet. The mob will then scatter, with only mothers and their joeys staying together.

Because adult male kangaroos are large animals, they have no natural predators. However, joeys may be snatched up by large birds of prey such as the wedge-tailed eagle. Joeys and small females are also preyed upon by packs of wild dogs called dingoes. The lead dingo will often chase the kangaroo toward its pack mates, which hide and wait for the kangaroo. Then they leap on the kangaroo and bite its neck.

Kangaroos are safe from dingoes only in Tasmania, where none of the predators exist.

A mob's dominant male usually holds his position for only one year before being forced out by a stronger male that challenges him.

A male begins courting by making clicking sounds that soothe and attract a female.

The Kangaroo Conservation Center in Dawsonville, Georgia, houses the largest public collection of kangaroos outside Australia.

Kangaroos defend themselves with clawed swipes and kicks that can tear a dingo apart. Kangaroos may also allow dingoes to chase them into a body of water. There a kangaroo will grab the dingo in its front paws and hold it underwater until it drowns. However, if a pack works together to attack a kangaroo, the dogs are often successful in bringing it down.

Male kangaroos kick and punch for a different reason. Kangaroos play-fight in order to show each other their skill and strength in a non-threatening way, but when the time comes for mating, males fight seriously to win a female. Fighting kangaroos swipe and jab with their forearms to knock their opponents off balance. They may also lean back on their tails and raise their rear legs up to deliver powerful kicks. When one kangaroo has had enough, he will retreat, leaving the winner with his choice of females.

Female kangaroos are choosy about potential mates. When approached, a female may swat many suitors away before allowing one of the right size and healthy appearance to court her. The female stands still as the male begins making clicking sounds close to her head. Then he will stroke her chest, neck, and tail. If she is

displeased, the female will hop away, but if she likes the male, she will allow him to mate with her.

Kangaroos have no specific mating season and breed all year round. Females have one joey at a time. After a **gestation** of 29 to 38 days, a joey the length and weight of a single paper clip is born. It is pink, hairless, and blind, yet it already has clawed front paws and a good sense of smell, which it uses immediately. Clutching its mother's fur and following its nose, the joey takes about three minutes to drag itself from its mother's birth canal

Punching with the front legs is a fairly harmless alternative to kangaroos "boxing" with their clawed hind legs.

When one kangaroo perceives a threat, other members of the mob will immediately look around for danger as well.

to the inside of her pouch, which is called a marsupium. There it clamps its mouth around one of her four teats, and the mother pumps milk down the joey's throat. The joey nurses for about three months, growing very slowly. Eventually, the mother's milk changes to include more protein and fat. This makes the joey grow more quickly.

Wallaroo and red kangaroo joeys are old enough to leave the pouch at about six months of age. Grey kangaroo joeys spend an additional two months in the pouch. Once they leave the pouch to begin feeding on grass, they can still easily jump back into the pouch for protection and to continue feeding on their mother's milk, which they will need for an additional six to eight months. When wallaroos and red kangaroos are 1 year old and grey kangaroos are 18 months old, they become independent of their mothers. By the time female red and grey kangaroos are 14 to 18 months old, they will be old enough to mate and have joeys of their own.

In all species of kangaroo except the western grey, reproduction is tied to the climate in which the kangaroos live. During times of drought, when vegetation is scarce, a female kangaroo that becomes pregnant while still

Small joeys are unable to regulate their own body temperatures and rely on their mothers to keep them warm.

A female kangaroo can have a joey outside the pouch but still nursing, a tiny joey in the pouch, and an undeveloped joey awaiting birth.

carrying a joey in her pouch may put the new baby "on hold" until her current joey leaves the pouch. During this period, called embryonic diapause, the **embryo** stops developing for up to 11 months until environmental conditions improve. This suspension of birth ensures that the new joey will have a food source when it is ready to eat grass. When the second joey is born and crawls into its mother's pouch, it is fed the kind of milk that newborns need, while the first joey, returning to the pouch only to nurse, is fed the kind of milk that older joeys need.

When food is in short supply, kangaroos cannot spend their days lounging in the shade and their nights nibbling on grass. Instead, they must constantly search for food, and this often leads them to cities and towns. Places that are watered—parks, lawns, golf courses, sports fields—are places where kangaroos will gather. And when such places are the only green environments available, kangaroos will refuse to be chased away.

Over a normal kangaroo's lifespan of 12 to 18 years in the wild (which can be shorter or longer, depending on food supply) or up to 25 years in captivity, a kangaroo may become accustomed to sharing its environment with

people. Kangaroos may appear tame around people, but they are wild animals that can grow to be as big and as heavy as an adult man, making them dangerous. People have been swatted, clawed, and kicked by kangaroos that are behaving only as they would against predators in the wild. Even pets can come into deadly contact with kangaroos, which view dogs, especially, as threats.

As cities have grown, kangaroos' fear of humans has decreased, and they approach populated areas without hesitation.

Aborigines taught a variety of
kangaroo hunting techniques
to early visitors to Australia.

BOUNCING OFF THE WALLS

Kangaroos have been a major part of Aboriginal culture since the first people arrived on the continent from Asia about 45,000 years ago. The native peoples had formed about 700 tribes that spoke more than 200 different languages by the time the first Europeans visited Australia in the late 1700s. The early Aborigines, who had more than 40 different names for the kangaroo, lived as hunter-gatherers. The women collected fruits, berries, plants, and bird eggs, and the men hunted large, flightless birds called emus, geese, and a variety of mammals as food sources. Small kangaroo relatives, including wallabies and bettongs, were caught with **snares** made of grass rope. Kangaroos were hunted with boomerangs, which are also called throwsticks.

A boomerang is a flat wooden weapon carved like a bent stick. A skilled boomerang thrower can knock a kangaroo—even a large boomer—off its feet. The name "boomerang" is an Aboriginal word. Locations where kangaroos were regularly hunted were called *kangaloola*. None of the kangaroo was wasted. Its meat was either cooked or dried in the sun and made into jerky. Its bones

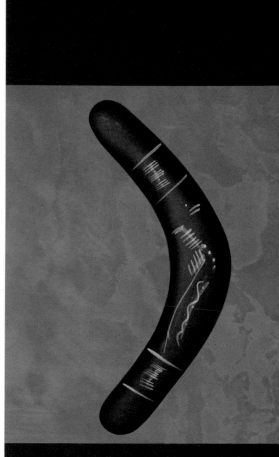

A 30,000-year-old boomerang led scientists to believe that boomerangs were the first heavier-than-air flying objects.

Aboriginal art often depicts ancestor spirits from the Dreamtime, the indigenous peoples' creation story.

Aboriginal farmers burned dry, grassy areas to promote the growth of new grass and keep kangaroos living nearby.

were made into tools, weapons, and sewing needles. The tendons from its tail were used as thread to sew clothing made from the kangaroo's hide and the skins of other animals. Kangaroo hides were also used as blankets and rugs, and they were made into bags for storing water.

The native peoples of Australia also included the kangaroo in their storytelling and religion. The early Aborigines had no written language. Instead, they used images to document stories. They painted and **stenciled** images of people and animals on rock faces and cave walls using charcoal, white clay, and ochre. Yellow and red ochre are **pigments** made from clay. All across Australia, more than 100,000 Aboriginal rock art sites have been discovered.

The oldest kangaroo paintings ever discovered exist in Kakadu National Park, east of the seaside city of Darwin in Australia's Northern Territory. The cave paintings in Kakadu are more than 10,000 years old. About 100 miles (161 km) from the city of Sydney, the capital of New South Wales, in the far southeastern corner of Australia, a 4,000-year-old Aboriginal rock art site was discovered in 2003. Not far from that site, more than 200 individual images—including those of lizards, birds, wombats, and

kangaroos—were found in a recently explored area of
Wollemi National Park. Also painted on the rock faces
are figures called therianthropes (*thee-ree-ANTH-ropes*).
These are half-human, half-animal figures. Some of the
therianthropes show humans with bird heads, and some
show human-like kangaroos.

These figures were tied into the many religious beliefs
about animals that were held by the Aborigines. Each
tribe had a **totem** that symbolized its connection to its
ancestors and to the land. The Aborigines believed that the
spirits of their ancestors lived in the totem animals of their
tribe. Some totems were plants, and some were animals.
Emus were common totems, as were kangaroos. If a man

Because ancient Aboriginal groups were so geographically scattered, they developed unique styles in rock art.

THE SING-SONG OF OLD MAN KANGAROO

This is the mouth-filling song
Of the race that was run by a Boomer,
Run in a single burst—only event of its kind—
Started by big God Nqong from Warrigaborrigarooma,
Old Man Kangaroo first: Yellow-Dog Dingo behind.

Kangaroo bounded away,
His back-legs working like pistons—
Bounded from morning till dark,
Twenty-five feet to a bound.
Yellow-Dog Dingo lay
Like a yellow cloud in the distance—
Much too busy to bark.
My! but they covered the ground!

Nobody knows where they went,
Or followed the track that they flew in,
For that Continent
Hadn't been given a name.
They ran thirty degrees,
From Torres Straits to the Leeuwin
(Look at the Atlas, please),
And they ran back as they came.

S'posing you could trot
From Adelaide to the Pacific,
For an afternoon's run
Half what these gentlemen did
You would feel rather hot,
But your legs would develop terrific—
Yes, my importunate son,
You'd be a Marvellous Kid!

From "The Sing-Song of Old Man Kangaroo,"
by Rudyard Kipling (1865–1936)

identified with kangaroos, he was called a kangaroo man. In most tribes, the rules regarding totems said that a kangaroo man could not eat kangaroo meat that was bloody. It had to be thoroughly cooked before he could eat it. In some kangaroo tribes, killing kangaroos was forbidden.

Aborigines have also inhabited Australia's neighboring island state, Tasmania, for thousands of years. One group of people call themselves the Palawa, which means "first man" in their language. They believe that a creation spirit made humans from a kangaroo. Long ago, people wore no clothing except a kangaroo skin draped over their shoulders like a poncho, and they painted their bodies with a mixture of ochre and bird fat. Even though the Palawa people hunted kangaroos and wallabies, they respected these animals, showing their appreciation for a killed animal's sacrifice with prayers and dances.

A popular myth about the kangaroo's discovery by 18th-century Europeans tells that when British captain James Cook visited Australia in 1770, he pointed to a kangaroo and asked an Aborigine what it was. The Aborigine supposedly said, "Kangaroo," which supposedly meant "I don't know" in his language. While this story has been

Along with Aborigines, modern companies such as the Qantas airline use kangaroos as identifying symbols.

Since 1965, more than 14 billion coins have been made at the Royal Australian Mint in the Canberra suburb of Deakin.

In the 1800s, Europeans living in Australia discovered that the tendons from a kangaroo's tail could be made into surgical thread.

proven false, the myth persists, and many people still believe that kangaroos are named for the phrase "I don't know." In truth, Captain Cook did visit Australia in 1770 after his ship, the *Endeavour*, ran aground on a coral reef and needed repairs before returning to sea. Aboard Cook's ship was the naturalist Joseph Banks, who recorded his impressions of the kangaroos he saw and learned the true Aboriginal name for the animal—*gungurru*.

Europeans quickly discovered the **commercial** value of kangaroos and began hunting them for their skins and meat. Although their numbers dropped drastically in the 1800s, kangaroos have always steadily reproduced and have, over the generations, been able to maintain a healthy population across most parts of Australia. As white settlements grew and cities developed in the 19th century, the kangaroo became a part of the art and architecture. Kangaroo gargoyles appeared atop buildings, images of kangaroos adorned windows and doors, and kangaroo statues were carved out of stone and cast out of metal to decorate parks and city centers.

People's regard for the kangaroo as a symbol of Australia's unique wildlife remains strong today. Australia's

coat of arms includes a kangaroo and an emu, symbols of the nation's natural heritage and progression toward the future because kangaroos and emus, unable to move backward, always move forward. Leaping kangaroos—the enduring symbol of Australia's optimistic attitude—serve as the emblems of Australia's military branches, the Qantas airline, and a number of Australian coins. The newest such coins, a set of eight gold coins released in 2009, bear the image of Queen Elizabeth II of England, the ruler of Australia, on the front. On the back, three of the coins show a leaping kangaroo, while the remaining five feature a kangaroo with a joey in its pouch.

The coat of arms created in 1908 was revised in 1912 to include the symbols of the six Australian states on the shield.

In 1994, scientists discovered the Wallal virus, which causes blindness in three percent of kangaroos that contract it.

PALS OR PESTS?

T he oldest known kangaroo ancestor was the size of a chipmunk. *Sinodelphys szalayi* was a marsupial that lived in China about 125 million years ago. It ran on all fours and ate insects and worms like modern opossums. About 25 million years ago, as kangaroo ancestors grew larger, they developed fangs and may have climbed trees. The first true kangaroos—hopping animals that resemble modern kangaroos—emerged in Australia about 15 million years ago. For millions of years, the giant short-faced kangaroo (*Procoptodon goliah*) dominated Australia's plains and forests. It stood 10 feet tall (3 m) and had massive claws and sharp hooves. It existed until just about 40,000 years ago, when a major drought led to a mass extinction of most of Australia's large animals and birds. Kangaroos grew smaller to survive and eventually became the animals we know today.

Kangaroos are legally protected in all territories of Australia, but for decades, these animals have been the subject of much disagreement among lawmakers, citizens, and conservationists. Some people see kangaroos

The giant short-faced kangaroo may have moved at slower speeds than modern kangaroos.

Over the past 40,000 years, the kangaroo's teeth gradually shortened to their present size, making them two-thirds the size of kangaroo ancestors'.

Kangaroos press their tails to the ground to balance themselves while grazing.

Eastern grey kangaroos are called foresters for their forest habitat, and western grey kangaroos are called stinkers for their smell.

as a **nuisance** animal that must be controlled. Others see Australia's national symbol as a valuable part of the **ecosystem** that must be preserved. Still others appreciate kangaroos for their commercial value. Scientific study and wildlife management programs function to create a balance between the need to control kangaroo populations and the need to protect the animals from senseless slaughter.

Many sheep farmers consider kangaroos a nuisance because their animals have to compete with kangaroos for grazing grass. A study conducted by the University of New South Wales in Sydney revealed that kangaroos have no negative effects on sheep farms—yet sheep farmers are legally allowed to shoot kangaroos that come onto their land. In urban areas, kangaroos can pose a danger to people. Since 1990, kangaroos in Australia's capital city of Canberra have outnumbered people 3 to 1, and more than 500 kangaroo-caused automobile accidents are reported each year. Other cities across Australia must also contend with ever-growing populations of kangaroos.

In Canberra, researchers are hoping to develop kangaroo management strategies by studying the home territory and movement patterns of urban kangaroos.

In 2009, 24 kangaroos were fitted with electronic collars designed to gather data on kangaroo movement over a period of 2 years. Each collar has a **Global Positioning System** (GPS) device that records the animal's position as it moves. The kangaroos were shot with a tranquilizer dart, fitted with a collar, and then released. The collars were designed to fall off after two years, at which time researchers could retrieve the collars and study the data.

A method of population control that provides immediate results is culling, or killing off a portion of the kangaroo population. Australia's citizens are divided on the issue, though. Some, such as farmers and ranchers, want to see kangaroos destroyed, while others want the government to come up with a better way of dealing with the overpopulation. Wildlife conservationists have filed legal complaints against the Australian government, calling the kangaroo culling cruel and unnecessary. Plans to cull large numbers of kangaroos within cities are often halted by public protest, yet most urban areas in Australia still regularly (and discreetly) remove kangaroos—either by trapping and relocating them or by shooting them.

Another method employed to decrease kangaroo

Kangaroos are smarter and easier to train than dogs, but they are also more independent and difficult to control.

Kangaroos are genetically resistant to ticks, and scientists are studying kangaroo genes to try to duplicate the resistance in livestock.

populations involves the commercial wildlife trade. Many companies in Australia are allowed to shoot kangaroos and sell their hides and meat. The number of kangaroos that can be "harvested" depends each year on the number of kangaroos counted by kangaroo management groups funded by the government. Since 1978, various groups have flown small airplanes over kangaroo habitats and counted the kangaroos in given areas. Then a percentage of that total count is declared to be the annual quota, or maximum number of kangaroos that can be killed for commercial purposes in that year.

Over the past 25 years, populations of kangaroos have **fluctuated** between 15 and 50 million. During times of fair weather and plenty of rainfall, kangaroos are abundant, and quotas are set high. In times of drought, kangaroo populations may plummet, and quotas are set low. In recent years, because of a drought that had plagued much of Australia, the annual quotas were set between 2 and 3 million, or roughly 15 percent of the kangaroo population. In 2009, the drought subsided, and the quota was set at four million. On average, only about 70 percent of the kangaroos that are allowed to be harvested are actually killed.

The animals that are harvested support an industry that generates more than $200 million per year. Australia exports kangaroo meat and skins to more than 55 nations around the world. Some researchers have even suggested that kangaroo meat may one day replace beef as the most popular meat product. Kangaroo skins are used in leather products, including soccer shoes, golf gloves, and baseball mitts. Kangaroo leather products are labeled as K leather or RKT, which stands for rubberized kangaroo technology.

Another field in which kangaroos are useful is human medical research. The Kangaroo Genome Project is

Kangaroos have adapted to recognize that cattle and sheep ranches are good places to find water in times of drought.

About 400 different Aboriginal groups exist in Australia, including the Koori, Luritja, and Arrernte peoples.

run by the ARC Centre of Excellence for Kangaroo Genomics, or KanGO, in Australia. Several Australian universities and research organizations make up KanGO, which has been researching kangaroo **genetics** since 2004. Some of the studies conducted are designed to learn more about human embryo and **fetus** development. Because kangaroo infants form outside the mother's body, this makes them the easiest of mammal fetuses to observe.

KanGO is also examining the possibility of duplicating kangaroo genes and inserting them into dairy cows to help them produce more milk, since kangaroos produce highly rich milk for their growing offspring. Kangaroo milk also contains powerful **antibiotics** that protect joeys from illness. Scientists are working toward an understanding of these substances with the goal of duplicating them for human use.

Kangaroos are cherished symbols of Australia, the unique "Land Down Under." Apart from providing endless entertainment for tourists, kangaroos serve many other valuable roles in human society. Proper management of kangaroo populations will ensure that Australia's boomers and flyers will always have a special land to call home.

Many vehicles in Australia are fitted with roo-bars, heavy metal hood attachments that offer protection against collisions with kangaroos.

ANIMAL TALE: WHY THE KANGAROO JUMPS

The kangaroo is an integral part of the Aborigines' culture. It is part of their music, their artwork, and their storytelling. This Aboriginal tale explains why the kangaroo jumps instead of runs and how the animal learned to survive being hunted by humans.

Long ago, the kangaroo crept along on all fours like the dingo. He browsed for grass and leaves on the plains and in the forests. Then humans arrived in Australia, hungry for the meat of animals. They had boomerangs that no four-legged animal could outrun. Kangaroo and the other animals feared humans because of this powerful weapon.

One day, as Kangaroo rested after a tasty breakfast, he heard something approaching through the brush. Kangaroo leaped to his feet just in time to see a man standing before him. The man had a boomerang in his hand, and he was looking straight at Kangaroo.

Kangaroo took off running as fast as he could. The man followed, chasing him across the plains. Then the man threw the boomerang. Kangaroo ducked low just in time to see the boomerang whiz past his face, make a wide arc in the sky, and then return to the man's hand. More terrified than ever, Kangaroo ran faster, but the man stayed right behind him.

Finally, the setting sun offered Kangaroo some relief. In the darkness, he was able to hide in the grass. But Kangaroo knew that the man had not gone far. In the morning, the man would kill him with the boomerang. Afraid and exhausted, Kangaroo curled up with his long tail and fell asleep.

A little while later, Kangaroo awoke to the sound of crackling

wood and the smell of smoke. The man had made a campfire and sat before it, stretching his hands toward its warmth. The man was very close to Kangaroo, but Kangaroo knew that if he moved, the man would spot him. It was no good. There seemed to be no escape.

Kangaroo slept and dreamed of the man, considering how he moved. He ran on two legs instead of four, yet he did not fall behind in chasing Kangaroo. *Perhaps two legs are better than four*, Kangaroo dreamed. When the sun came up, Kangaroo knew he had to move. Swallowing his fear, Kangaroo suddenly jumped up and raised himself on his two hind legs. He tried to run, but he could not put one leg in front of the other. The man spotted Kangaroo and reached for his boomerang.

In a burst of fear and energy, Kangaroo threw both his hind legs forward at the same time, making a great leap. Then he did it again and again. Balancing with his long tail, he jumped farther and farther. The man tried to follow, but he could not match Kangaroo's long leaps. The man threw his boomerang, but Kangaroo jumped right over it as it flew past him. Soon, Kangaroo had left the man far behind.

This is the best way to move, Kangaroo thought. He showed all of the other kangaroos how to jump on their hind legs. Soon the front legs of the kangaroos became smaller, and the hind legs grew bigger. This is why, today, a kangaroo can leap straight over the top of a man's head and leave him far behind in just a few bounds.

GLOSSARY

Aboriginal – of or relating to the Australian Aborigines, the people who inhabited Australia before the arrival of European settlers

adapted – changed to improve its chances of survival in its environment

antibiotics – medicines that kill or disable the growth of bacteria, or living organisms that cannot be seen except under a microscope

Australasian – of Australia, New Zealand, or the islands northeast of Australia

coat of arms – the official symbol of a family, state, nation, or other group

commercial – used for business and to gain a profit rather than for personal reasons

ecosystem – a community of organisms that live together in an environment

embryo – an unborn or unhatched offspring in its early stages of development

evaporates – changes from liquid to invisible vapor or gas

fetus – an unborn offspring of a mammal that has all its features (limbs, organs, eyes, etc.) and a basic resemblance to the adult

fluctuated – rose and fell in an irregular number or amount

genetics – the biological origins of traits or characteristics

gestation – the period of time it takes a baby to develop inside its mother's womb

Global Positioning System – a system of satellites, computers, and other electronic devices that work together to determine the location of objects or living things that carry a trackable device

hierarchy – a system in which people, animals, or things are ranked in importance one above another

nuisance – something annoying or harmful to people or the land

pigments – materials or substances present in the tissues of animals or plants that give them their natural coloring

snares – traps for small animals that have a noose made of wire or rope

stenciled – painted or marked around a sheet of material that has been cut in a certain shape

sterile – incapable of producing offspring

tendons – tough, inelastic tissues that connect muscle to bone

totem – an object, animal, or plant respected as a symbol of a tribe and often used in ceremonies and rituals

SELECTED BIBLIOGRAPHY

Dawson, Terence J. *Kangaroos: Biology of the Largest Marsupials.* Sacramento: Comstock Publishing, 1995.

Department of Foreign Affairs and Trade. "Kangaroos," Australian Government. http://www.dfat.gov.au/facts/kangaroos.html.

Dickman, Christopher, and Rosemary Woodford Ganf. *A Fragile Balance: The Extraordinary Story of Australian Marsupials.* Chicago: University of Chicago Press, 2008.

Kangaroo Industry Association of Australia. "How the Kangaroo Industry Works." KIAA. http://www.kangaroo-industry.asn.au/industry.html.

McCullough, Dale R., and Yvette McCullough. *Kangaroos in Outback Australia.* New York: Columbia University Press, 2000.

Watts, Dave. *Kangaroos & Wallabies of Australia.* Chatswood, New South Wales, Australia: New Holland Publishers, 1999.

Kangaroos may hop along a beach or into shallow water but do not venture far unless they are trying to escape a predator.

INDEX

antilopine kangaroos 11, 17

body temperature control 11

conservation measures and studies 22, 37, 38, 39, 40, 41, 43
    genetics research 40, 41, 43
    Kangaroo Conservation Center 22
    legal protections 37
    monitoring 39
    relocation 39
    wildlife management 38

cultural influences 29–31, 33–35, 38, 43, 44
    on Aboriginal arts 30, 31, 44
    on Aboriginal religion 30, 31, 33
    symbolic importance 34–35, 38, 43
    on urban art and architecture 34

dangerous to humans 27, 38

diet 7, 15, 16–17, 18, 25, 44
    and digestion 16–17
    vegetation 7, 15, 16, 17, 18, 25, 44

first Europeans in Australia 29, 33, 34
    Captain James Cook 33, 34

grey kangaroos 11, 15, 17, 18, 25, 38
    eastern 11, 15, 38
    western 11, 15, 25, 38

grooming 19

habitats 7, 11, 12, 17, 18, 25, 26–27, 29, 30, 33, 34, 37, 38, 39,
    40, 44
    Australia 7, 11, 12, 17, 18, 29, 30, 34, 37, 39, 44
    climates 12, 25, 40
        droughts 25, 40
    forests 18, 38, 44
    islands 11, 12, 33
        Tasmania 33
    plains 17, 44
    urban settings 26–27, 38, 39

home territories 18, 38

joeys 7–8, 21, 23, 25, 26, 35, 43
    appearance at birth 23
    and embryonic diapause 26
    fetus development 43
    independence from mothers 25
    nursing on milk 25, 26, 43

kangaroo leather products 41

life expectancy 26

Macropodidae family 11

mating 18, 22–23, 25

movement 11, 18, 19, 35, 37, 38, 39, 44, 45
    patterns of 38, 39

names for kangaroos 11, 12, 15, 29, 43
    Aboriginal 11, 29
    females 12, 15, 43
    males 12, 15, 29, 43

national parks 7, 30, 31

physical characteristics 7, 8, 11, 12, 15–16, 18, 19, 21, 22,
    23, 25, 26, 30, 35, 37, 44, 45
    claws 19, 22, 23
    coloration 15
    feet 11, 18, 19, 21
    fur 15, 23
    legs 18, 19, 22, 45
    paws 18, 19, 22, 23
    pouches 7, 8, 12, 25, 26, 35
    sizes 12, 15
    tails 11, 18, 22, 30, 44, 45
    teeth 11, 15–16, 30, 37

populations 34, 38, 39, 40, 41, 43
    control of 38, 39, 43
    harvested for wildlife trade 40, 41

predators 8, 19, 21, 22, 27, 29, 33, 34, 44
    birds of prey 8, 21
    defense against 19, 22
    dingoes 21, 22
    hunting by humans 29, 33, 34, 44

red kangaroos 11, 12, 15, 17, 18, 25

relatives 11, 12, 29, 30, 33, 37
    ancestors 30, 37
    macropods 11, 29, 33
    marsupials 12, 30

roles of males and females 21, 22
    dominant males 21
    matriarchs 21

sleeping 7, 18

social behaviors 21, 22
    communication 22
    living in mobs 21
    play-fighting 22

speeds 18

wallaroos 11, 15, 18, 25
    black 11
    common 11